Boise State University Western Writers Series   Number 90

David Henry Hwang

By Douglas Street

Bryan, Texas

D0921962

Editors: Wayne Chatterton
James H. Maguire

Business Manager:
James Hadden

Cover Design and Illustration by
Arny Skov, Copyright 1989

Boise State University, Boise, Idaho

Library of Congress Card No. 89-60059

International Standard Book No. 0-88430-089-7

Printed in the United States of America by
Boise State University Printing and Graphics Services
Boise, Idaho

David Henry Hwang

David Henry Hwang

I am much better now . . . . My parents—they don't know nothing about the world, about watching Benson at the Roxy, . . . downshifting onto the Ventura Freeway at midnight. They're yellow ghosts and they've tried to cage me up with Chinese-ness when all the time we were in America. So, I've had to work real hard—real hard—to be myself. To not be a Chinese, a yellow, a slant, a gook. To be just a human being, like everyone else. I've paid my dues. And that's why I am much better now. I'm making it, you know? I'm making it in America. (*FOB* 36)

Traditionally, the predominant images of the Asian and the Asian-American in popular culture have been created and exploited by Westerners. This historical evolution of the "coolie" laborer and laundryman, Bret Harte's so-called "heathen Chinee'," has largely resulted from Old West myth-making. The Chinese railroad worker of the last century hammered together America's backbone while his own was being broken. Yet generations of Asian-Americans have chosen to forget this heritage. As articulated above by playwright David Henry Hwang, it stands as an obstacle to assimilation into the majority culture. Instead they risk becoming "yellow ghosts," trapped within stereotypes, the perpetual "Hop Sings" of the American "Ponderosa." But for Hwang and a new generation of Asian-American voices, the keys to unlock the vitality of their heritage are to be found in the American West—the railroad, the

Mother Lode, the bygone joss houses in gold rush towns like Chinese Camp. In these lie the Oriental heritage and the anguish of forgotten Western American trailblazers.

From the writings of Bret Harte, Samuel Clemens, and others emerged a caricature of the Chinese that clearly locked them into the "yellow ghost" stereotype. As the caricature moved from fiction onto film, it evolved too. White filmgoers of the thirties and forties welcomed the screen portrayals of Earl Derr Biggers' "noble Chinee'" Charlie Chan. Ever-perceptive and ultra-humble, he was a Western lawman of a different sort who rounded up outlaws of the New West. Though positive in many ways, Chan was still a caricature, created by a white, portrayed by a white, for a predominantly white film-going audience.

In the playhouses, a pseudo-Oriental image was popularized for Anglo-American theatergoers early in this century. For many, *Madame Butterfly*, the Belasco play and the Puccini opera, was the quintessential love story. The post-World War II interest in the mystique of the Far East fostered such Anglo-oriented successes as *The King and I, Teahouse of the August Moon,* and *Flower Drum Song.* It was not until the 1960s that Asian-American writers, in all genres, began to break traditionally white artistic barriers with truly Asian-inspired literature.

One of the first and most influential Asian-American playwrights and theatrical directors was Frank Chin. His plays of the early 1970s—*Chickencoop Chinaman, Year of the Dragon,* and *Gee, Pop!*— cracked theater's longstanding Asian barriers. Though not commercially successful nor universally acclaimed, Chin's writings nevertheless pointed the way for other emerging dramatists. The effort and guidance of Chin and his colleagues spurred the formation of several Asian-American theater companies in the West and in New York. The East/West Players, the Asian American Theatre Com-

6

pany, and others in turn encouraged and developed new Asian-American plays, players, and playwrights. Thus, a partial solution was being offered for the inherent problem facing Oriental dramatists—traditionally, white producers have been reluctant to finance an Asian-oriented production for their majority Anglo audiences. Unlike black drama, Oriental culture seems alien to long-held occidental values, and hence its dramas have generally fared poorly at the box-office. Frank Chin was a visible pioneer, yet not until the companies developed their own talents did a host of dynamic playwrights turn inward for relevant material, to explore on stage the "Asian-ness" in the American and the "American-ness" in the Asian, and to consciously dramatize the joys, sorrows, and complexities of growing up Asian-American in the New American West.

Of all the playwrights theatrically exploring these themes, one artist has dominated the medium—the Californian David Henry Hwang. Within the decade following the success of his first dramatic attempt, Hwang had five major productions in New York and abroad. In addition, out of these six Hwang garnered four off-Broadway "Best Play" nominations and awards, while the sixth, his first play for Broadway, won both the New York Drama Desk and Tony Awards for best Broadway play of 1987-88. At thirty-two, David Hwang became the most successful, most acclaimed Asian-American playwright in American theater history. More significantly, he was the first to successfully transcend the theatrical boundaries between white and Oriental without compromising his own concerns and dramatic themes. His awards have been meted out by predominantly white panels; his box-office success has been from predominantly white theatergoers. In his work Asia and America come together with the piquancy of a Los Angeles Chinese restaurant, the force of a Chinese road gang laying track through the Sierras, the grace of Tai-chi and the Peking Opera performed on a San Francisco afternoon.

David Henry Hwang (pronounced "Wong") was born in 1957, in San Gabriel, California, a Los Angeles suburb. His father, Henry Y. Hwang, grew up in Shanghai, China, and emigrated in the late 1940s to California, where he enrolled in the University of Southern California's business program. While studying at U.S.C., he met his wife-to-be, Dorothy. Hwang's mother was born in Amoy in southeast China but was reared in the Philippines. She was a talented musician from a prosperous Chinese family. In 1952, her parents sent her to U.S.C. to further her ambition to become a concert pianist. At U.S.C. Hwang's parents met and eventually married. Though both received degrees, Dorothy relinquished her dreams of a concert career to raise David and his two younger sisters. Hwang's father became first a C.P.A., then a dabbler in various business ventures from the founding of his own accounting firm to the managing of the Imperial Garden Restaurant in Hollywood. The senior Hwang went on to found and preside over the Far East National Bank in Los Angeles, the first federally chartered Asian-American bank in the United States. As her children grew older and more independent, Dorothy became a successful piano instructor in Los Angeles.

David Hwang recalled, in an interview for Hong Kong's *South China Morning Post*, "My father came from Shanghai and my mother was Philippino Chinese. They spoke English in the home; they wanted to assimilate, and wanted their children to assimilate. Nevertheless, they were torn" (2 Dec. 1982: 11). David and his sisters were enrolled for a time in Chinese language classes in Los Angeles, but they were eventually withdrawn because their parents feared such classes might hamper their children's English studies. "My father has always been interested in discarding the past," said

8

Hwang in a recent interview. "He's never much liked China, or the whole idea behind China or Chinese ways of thinking. He's always been much more attracted to American ways of thinking" (Gerard 88).

San Gabriel was a solid, multi-ethnic California community when Hwang lived there. "In school there were a lot of Asians and Hispanics. I didn't have much ethnic consciousness at the time. I recognized I was Chinese, but it was no more different than having red hair" (Christon 4). What the young Hwang learned of China and the Chinese came primarily from relatives and from contacts within the family's "born again" Evangelical Christian Church involvement. Hwang and other Chinese-Americans growing up in the West tend to "grow up thinking of ourselves as Caucasians. But when new immigrants arrive, it throws into relief the Chinese sides of us that we try to ignore" (*South China Post* 11).

Hwang's childhood was a typical California suburban experience. Under his mother's guidance, he developed his musical talents. Beginning the violin at age seven, Hwang blossomed into a solid virtuoso. His equal expertise in debate won his enrollment into Harvard Boys School, a rather exclusive boys' preparatory school in the Hollywood Hills. At Harvard, Hwang honed his speaking and debating skills with an eye toward becoming a lawyer. Theater and playwriting were not in his plans. It was not until Hwang had been at Harvard for awhile that he saw his first play. Susan Dietz, an English teacher at the school, mounted a production of Arthur Kopit's play *Indians*, his symbolic presentation of the downfall of the American Indian at the hands of a white America personified by Buffalo Bill and his Wild West Show. From that production young Hwang gained an early appreciation for "the collaborative effort of the stage that forces you to expand," and for "theater's accessibility, which makes it easier to explore spiritual states and differing consciousnesses" (Christon 4). Though intriguing, a theater career was not a possibility when he graduated from Harvard Boys and entered Stanford University in the fall of 1975, still intent upon studying law.

By the end of his second year at Stanford, Hwang felt an urge to write plays. He still cannot explain it precisely, but it led to Stanford creative writing professor, John L'Heureux. At the time, Hwang had still read few plays and had seen fewer. He recalled L'Heureux's initial response to his playwriting desires:

"The desire to write plays in a vacuum is not enough," (counseled L'Heureux). "One must become actively involved in the theatrical process to get a feeling for how plays are different from other prose forms." I had (says Hwang) to realize that in playwriting the written word is not as important as the word spoken in the air. (Colker B1)

Heeding this advice, David Hwang began reading and attending as many plays as possible. During the summer of 1977, he won an internship at the East/West Players and subsequently spent the summer immersed in set construction, scene painting, and other odd jobs around the theater. He also observed the rehearsal process and the actors' development of characters. Back at Stanford for his junior year, Hwang continued his playgoing and commenced serious writing. He was particularly taken with the power and drama of Sam Shepard's avant-garde pieces for San Francisco's Magic Theater. In Shepard he found a role model who could combine human interaction and Western American mythmaking into explosive theater. Hwang confided he got "real intense" over the writing of Shepard. In 1978, the young playwright, now officially an English major, enrolled in the first Padua Hills Playwrights Festival workshop in Claremont, California, to study under Shepard and other Western American playwrights. It was during this workshop that the initial ideas for *FOB*, his first major play, surfaced. In November of 1978, the first drafts of *FOB* were composed. Stanford University annually involved interested living groups in a campus-wide performance festival of plays and musicals written and performed by the students. Hwang's *FOB* was selected to be the Okada House entry with Hwang doubling as stage director. The production, directed by Hwang and financed in part by the student-run Stanford Asian American Theatre Project, was first performed in the lounge of the Okada House dorm in March of 1979. Hwang did not tell his teachers about the performance, but he did invite his parents. His father had read the script and according to Hwang had been displeased by some of its coarse language:

> But he decided that he should come up to Stanford and see it staged to decide if this new interest of mine was something he could support. And so the entire family came up, and my father was very moved by the play and he cried. From that point on, my father decided my playwriting was something I should do and since then he's been very supportive. (Stayton E10)

At the same time, Hwang submitted *FOB* to the Playwrights' Conference of the O'Neill Theater Center in Waterford, Connecticut. Just before his graduation from Stanford he received word that the play would be one of twelve, chosen from over one thousand submitted, to be developed and produced at the O'Neill Conference that summer. Hwang left Stanford in June 1979, with a Bachelor's Degree in English, Phi Beta Kappa distinction, and a beginning playwriting career. Within a month he was developing *FOB* under the direction of Robert Ackerman, resident director for the New York Shakespeare Festival, part of producer Joseph Papp's organization. Thinking the piece held promise, Ackerman persuaded Hwang to permit him to show it to Papp. Joseph Papp

11

liked it, and in June 1980, he opened *FOB* at his NYSF Public Theater off-Broadway. Out of his O'Neill Conference experience, Hwang maintained, came an important lesson in how to "filter criticism." As he explained to Eric Pace of *The New York Times*, he realized that "I had written this play which knowledgeable and experienced people seemed to find enjoyable, and so I had best trust the instincts that created it in the first place" (12 July 1981: 4D).

The provocative *FOB* launched David Hwang's career. Inspired by the controversial Frank Chin play, *Gee, Pop!*, particularly its utilization of the Chinese folk hero Gwan Gung, and by the magnificent development of Fa Mu Lan (Maxine Hong Kingston's titular *Woman Warrior*), the then college senior fashioned a dramatic work at once wholly American in its style, Asian in its concerns. In his "Playwright's Note" to the play, published in *Broken Promises: Four Plays* (from which all *FOB* quotes are taken), Hwang introduces his play as "thoroughly American. The play began when a sketch I was writing about a limousine trip through Westwood, California, was invaded by two figures from American literature: Fa Mu Lan, the girl who takes her father's place in battle, . . . and Gwan Gung, the god of fighters and writers . . . the adopted god of Chinese America" (3). Hwang had read Kingston's 1976 bestseller and was excited in realizing as she had that it was possible to successfully "interweave the hyperrealistic details of contemporary American life with the larger, mythic ghost story in the background" (Gerard 88).

FOB is an acronym for "Fresh Off the Boat," a Chinese awash in America. The play is set in the back room of a small Chinese restaurant in Torrance, southern California. The time is now. The play is a pas de trois in which three characters weave in and out, confronting each other directly and indirectly, and raising questions and concerns which cut deeply across color lines and into the heart of personal identity. There is Grace, the first generation Chinese-American. She was born in Taiwan but has become Americanized since moving to Los Angeles at the age of ten. Dale is Grace's cousin and a second generation Chinese-American. Thoroughly American, he is a dues-paying member of the Sino-Angeleno brotherhood. Lastly, there is Steve, fresh off the boat from Hong Kong. Replete with a heavy Chinese accent, an Oriental demeanor, and a naiveté about the ways of the Asian-American West, he has come to study at U.C.L.A. All three are in their early twenties. Steve becomes the catalyst in this trio when physically and spiritually he forces Dale into a struggle with his "Chinese self."

For Dale, the FOB (Fresh Off the Boat) is the worst of Orientals to behold. In an ingenious prologue to the action Dale lectures to the audience on the "FOB phenomenon":

> F-O-B. Fresh Off the Boat. FOB. What words can you think of that characterize the FOB? Clumsy, ugly, greasy FOB. Loud, stupid, four-eyed FOB. Big feet. Horny. Like Lenny in *Of Mice and Men*. . . . Boy FOBs are the worst. . . . They are the sworn enemies of all ABC—oh, that's "American Born Chinese"—of all ABC girls. Before an ABC girl will be seen on Friday night with a boy FOB in Westwood, she would rather burn off her face. (7)

As the play begins, Dale not only is angered and disgusted by the new Chinese, the "FOB" stereotype, but he is equally in awe of one whose heritage is so remote yet so indelibly a part of his own cultural make-up. For Dale, this paradox leads to an overpowering frustration—no matter how "American" (that is, Caucasian) Dale feels or acts, on the outside he will always be "Chinese."

It is Grace who acts as a pivot for the two male sparring partners. Of the three characters, she possesses the best understanding of the plight of the newly-arrived Chinese and of the Americanized Chinese whose sole tie to "the Old Country" is a periodic drive into Chinatown, Los Angeles, or a movie at Mann's Chinese Theatre in Hollywood. It is to Grace that the audience must turn for guidance and understanding, because she is a formidable link between Sino and Anglo worlds. Into this early play Hwang injects what have become two central and pervading issues for him—the conflict between insiders and outsiders, and the plight of the lonely. Both issues seem to pose special problems for the Oriental in Occidental America. In a speech from *FOB*, Grace laments:

> Yeah. It's tough trying to live in Chinatown. But it's tough trying to live in Torrance, too. It's true. I don't like being alone. You know, when Mom could finally bring me to the U.S., I was already ten. But I never studied my English very hard in Taiwan, so I got moved back to the second grade. There were a few Chinese girls in the fourth grade, but they were American-born, so they wouldn't even talk to me. . . . I figured I had a better chance of getting in with the white kids than with them, so in junior high I started bleaching my hair and hanging out at the beach. . . . But the American-born Chinese, it didn't matter to them. They just giggled and went to their own dances. Until my senior year in high school—that's how long it took for me to get over this whole thing. (34)

Hwang has orchestrated Grace's monologue toward the audience while Steve and Dale, engrossed in petty rivalry, never hear. But Dale too is an outsider, an "ABC" in an Anglo land. "I've had to work real hard—real hard—to be myself. To not be a Chinese . . . . To be just a human being, like everyone else. . . . I'm making it, you know? I'm making it in America" (36).

The two-act drama begins in the back room of the restaurant

with Grace wrapping a package. Steve enters and announces himself as the great god "Gwan Gung." The two verbally spar until Grace informs him that in America, Gwan Gung is "dead." He is unknown, one that does not matter. But this exchange rekindles her own fantasy—Fa Mu Lan, the great woman warrior—in a sprightly, forceful monologue, before Dale enters the scene. Upon meeting Steve, Dale is quick to rebuke him for his manifestly "FOBish" characteristics, a rebuke that motivates Grace to act as mediator. The more "Gwan Gung" forces himself upon "the West," the more explosive the relationship between FOB and ABC becomes. Act One ends in Dale's blow-up and walk-out.

The second act begins with Dale's long monologue on his struggle to overcome his Chinese-ness. He has been superficially successful. Now, with Steve's intervention, Dale has been forced to reexamine his own identity in light of Steve's. Dale's attempt to humiliate the immigrant into subservience to the "American" leads to a powerful monologue wherein Steve becomes the embodiment of the "ChinaMan," the immigrant Everyman willfully undertaking menial labor in order to survive in the American West.

> This land does not want us any more than China. . . . All work was done, then the bosses said they could not send us back. . . . All America wants ChinaMen go home, but no one want it bad enough to pay our way. . . . I ask you, what you hate most? What work most awful for white woman? . . . Good. I will do that thing for you—you can give me food. (54)

The plight of the immigrant in the American West and the cultural kinship to a past submerged are finally the ties that bind Steve to Grace, "Gwan Gung" to "Fa Mu Lan." Grace's pronouncement transmutes Steve from dead god into living warrior. When these two exit together into the night, it is Dale who is left behind.

He sits amid the remnants of his ancestral culture unrepentant, uncomprehending. Dale ends the play as he began it—the "FOB" is reviled. But Dale's words now fall on an empty stage.

Public reaction to the play was overwhelmingly positive. Critics in New York, Los Angeles, and San Francisco all praised the depth and humanity of this initial script by the then twenty-two-year-old Hwang. While recognizing and appreciating its Chinese-American themes, critics and audiences alike found more universal, cross-cultural values and messages formulated within the drama.

> *FOB* reminded me of the "greenhorns," the Jews who came from Eastern Europe. Even though the cultures were strikingly different, it was the same notion. The principle of someone coming from the old country who didn't know how to behave was very much part of my own tradition. (Joseph Papp in Gerard 89)

Misha Berson of the *San Francisco Bay Guardian* found *FOB* "mystifying at first and you have to dig for it, but ultimately it yields rich and surprising rewards . . . . Like all successful works of art it transcends its particulars. It becomes a deeply meaningful play for all those whose roots in other cultures make them, no matter how 'assimilated,' strangers in a strange land" (13). The question of ethnic identity is one close to Hwang's heart. Growing up, Hwang himself experienced many of the same feelings toward immigrants to the West as does Dale in the play. He shares the feelings of Papp, Berson, and others who view his play as a metaphor for all immigrants in a new land. Interviewed in Los Angeles by the *Herald Examiner*'s Richard Stayton, Hwang recalled that concerns he felt unique to his own ethnicity were actually being shared by others and at many different levels. Even within other Asian groups Hwang discovered this cultural schizophrenia:

> Asian-Americans are always going, "We have to figure out

what our identity is. We're not quite white Americans and we're not quite Asian-Asians so we must be a third entity." And if you're in the states all the time you think it's a unique concern. But in Taiwan the Chinese were asking, "Are we Taiwanese or are we mainland Chinese?" In Singapore they were going, "Well, we don't quite know who we are, either." (E10)

While satisfied with the progress of the production, the young Californian could not cope with the city. Days before *FOB*'s off-Broadway opening, he returned to California. While elated with the play's success, and that of Mako, its director, and John Lone, its lead actor (as Steve), Hwang maintained his California residence. While *FOB* garnered prestigious awards—the 1980 Drama-Logue Playwriting Award, the 1981 U.S.-Asia Institute Award, the 1981 Obie Award for best off-Broadway production and another Obie for Lone as best actor—Hwang taught English and writing at Menlo-Atherton High School near his Stanford haunts, and prepared for entrance into Yale University's graduate playwriting program. It was while studying at Yale in late 1980, that Hwang began work on his next play, *The Dance and the Railroad.*

I wanted to try writing a historical play. For some time I had wanted to write a play about the work of Chinese-Americans on the transcontinental railroad, and I wanted to center it around a particular historical incident, the strike of 1867. . . . At the same time, though, it was important to me that this be a very personal play, that the Chinese-Americans not be presented as polemics but as people, and so I decided to focus on the relationship of two workers, and how they spend their time during this strike. And while the strike affects both of them, in the play it's a background, if omnipresent, event. (Pace 4D)

On the strength of *FOB*'s success, this second play was commissioned by the New Federal Theater in New York and initially funded by a grant from the Ethnic Heritage Studies Division of the U.S. Department of Education. As Maxine Kingston's *Woman Warrior* provided source material for the fleshing out of the Grace/Fa Mu Lan connection in *FOB*, so again did he turn to her for historic and mythic background in *The Dance and the Railroad*. In her second book, *China Men*, in "The Grandfather of the Sierra Nevada Mountains," Kingston chronicles the saga of her grandfather Ah Goong, as he built the railroad across Nevada and California and participated in the 1867 Chinese laborers' strike. Much of Hwang's character outline for his idealistic and gullible "Ma" in the play, as well as that character's fascination with the Chinese operatic folk hero Gwan Gung, attests to his assimilation of Kingston's stories. It is Kingston who first exposes as false the myth of the "coolie" laborers as stupid, spineless, and servile to the white bosses. Hwang explores and subsequently debunks this same misconception in *The Dance and the Railroad*. But as Hwang's *Dance* evolves, it increasingly eclipses political and historical issues with artistic ones heavily laden with the traditions of Chinese opera and culture. Their clash with Western values is as resounding as the labor strike played out unseen by us on the railroad down below. Though anchored in a historical context, this play, like the earlier *FOB*, treats the isolation and anxiety of the Asian immigrant in the American West.

In *The Dance and the Railroad*, the playwright sharpens his focus to develop the outsider "Lone." He is a refugee from the Chinese Opera, trained to portray Gwan Gung the mythic hero but now relegated to "coolie" status on the rail gang. While the workers strike below, Lone practices his art upon the mountainside above them. Ascending the heights in search of the artist is wide-eyed, gullible, "FOB" laborer Ma. Like Kingston's Ah Goong, he is full of the promises of "Gold Mountain." Like Ah Goong, he too searches for the mystic Gwan Gung among the Chinese camps of America. Their drama is stark yet captivating. Two men undergo an intellectual, physical, and artistic tug-of-war on the side of a mountain. The one player is worldly-wise and cynical. He defies his destruction through relentless adherence to his daily theatrical regimen. The other player is all too eager to believe the tales of "streets of gold" foisted on him by other "ChinaMen." Like Steve in *FOB*, Ma wishes to learn the opera to portray Gwan Gung in this new land.

The play is divided into five scenes, beginning on a June afternoon in 1867, the fourth day of the railroad strike, and progressing through the dawn of the eleventh strike day. In scene one, Ma encounters Lone in practice. We discover that Lone is ostracized by workers down below. Ma warns, "You gotta watch yourself. You know what they say? They call you 'Prince of the Mountain.' Like you're too good to spend time with them" (*Broken Promises* 64). Lone is unmoved. Ma retreats from this initial confrontation only to return the following afternoon. This second scene allows the playwright a vehicle for expounding upon the rigors involved in the actor-training process and upon the status of art and actors in Chinese society—"You don't know how you endanger your relatives by becoming an actor." Ma wishes to perform as Lone does but Lone challenges him:

Are you willing to come up after you've spent the whole day chipping half an inch off a rock, and punish your body some more? . . . It's ugly to practice when the mountain has turned your muscles to ice. When my body hurts too much to come here, I look at the other ChinaMen and think, "They are dead. Their muscles work only because the white man forces them. I live because I can still force my muscles to work for me." (73)

The scene ends with Lone reluctantly agreeing to accept Ma as a probationary student.

When scene three commences, four days have elapsed. Ma has begun to see the complexity of his undertaking, but his desire is still fueled by his dream of portraying Gwan Gung before his peers. But Ma must absorb the lesson painfully learned by Lone.

> It's not you. Everyone must earn the right to play Gwan Gung. I entered opera school when I was ten years old. My parents decided to sell me for ten years to this opera company. . . . After eight years, I was studying to play Gwan Gung. . . . I was one of the best in my class. One day I was summoned by my master, who told me I was to go home for two days, because my mother had fallen very ill and was dying. When I arrived home, Mother was standing at the door waiting, not sick at all. Her first words to me, the son away for eight years, were, "You've been playing while your village has starved. You must go to the Gold Mountain and work." . . . I went from a room with eighty boys to a ship with three hundred men. So, you see, it does not come easily to play Gwan Gung. (78)

Though debased and chastised, Ma good-naturedly perseveres. To prove his dedication he rises to Lone's challenge and spends the night on the mountain in his locust posture. Hwang provides wonderful insight into Ma's condition and into the "immigrant as locust" metaphor exploited throughout the later parts of the play. He devotes the short fourth scene to Ma's solo introspection upon his metamorphosis on the mount. Ma passes his ordeal and, on the day the strike is settled, wins approval to study Gwan Gung. This news begins the fifth and final scene. With the strike settled and the laborers winning their modified demands against the "White devils,"

Ma rejects Gwan Gung to return to work below and to resume his hunt for Western riches. As in Hwang's earlier play, the outsider chooses to confront his fears and comes down from the heights to do battle in the immediate world of the West. Just as Grace chooses Steve over Dale as the partner with whom to confront the Anglo world in *FOB*, so in *Dance* does Lone choose Ma. But while Steve goes as Ma goes, Lone will remain aloof on the mountain at least temporarily, hidden within his art as in the drama's beginning. He is Lone once again, content with himself at last—"Today, I am dancing for no reason at all" (98-99).

Much of the artistic credit for the evolution and development of the characters "Lone" and "Ma" must go directly to their namesakes, the two actors who originated the roles for the Henry Street Settlement's New Federal Theater and who carried them over to the off-Broadway NYSF Public Theater (the site of *FOB*'s success) four months later. Both actors John Lone and Tzi Ma were trained in Oriental theater and dance. The Obie winner as Steve in *FOB*, Lone developed a fruitful artistic relationship with Hwang, growing in stature as an actor as Hwang matured as a playwright. Lone had spent eight years in Hong Kong training with the Peking Opera Company before emigrating to the U.S. In a dual capacity he also directed *Dance*, embroidering meticulous dance and movement designs upon the rich fabric of Hwang's scripts. During the course of the initial Henry Street rehearsals, the artistic impact of John Lone and Tzi Ma was both valuable and unmistakable. Hwang lacked expertise in traditional drama and music. In Tzi Ma and especially John Lone, he had experts. Hwang acknowledged this to Eric Pace of *The New York Times*, who wrote that "much of the material in 'The Dance and the Railroad' he has taken from the lives of the Chinese-American actors who play the parts, John Lone and Tzi Ma—which is why their own real names appear in the play. They were in the cast of the Public's 'FOB' and in the first production of 'Dance' " (4D).

The Dance and the Railroad premiered at Henry Street Settlement's off-off-Broadway New Federal Theater, 25 March 1981, with direction, music, and choreography also by Lone. An immediate hit, the show was quickly picked up by Joseph Papp for his Public Theater. On July 16th, Hwang's company moved into Papp's Anspacher Theater for an extended run fueled by excited critical response and excellent box-office. Since the success of FOB, the New York theatrical community had been anxiously awaiting the next offering by the still inexperienced playwright. Would Hwang be a "one-play phenomenon" or would he be able to continue his success? The critical consensus after the opening of Dance was that David Hwang was indeed a playwright with a solid theatrical future. As critic Edith Oliver wrote in the 27 July 1981 issue of the New Yorker:

> Mr. Hwang has compressed into a play that lasts under an hour and a quarter the whole story of Chinese immigration in this country in the nineteenth century and again Mr. Lone is his hero. . . . Mr. Hwang . . . has written a play whose effect is nothing short of hypnotic. (52)

Douglas Watt of the New York Daily News (17 July 1981) concurred: "David Henry Hwang's hypnotic 'The Dance and the Railroad' . . . is a unique and lovely piece of theater. . . . The play is remarkable in its beauty and simplicity" (M6). The critic for New York Magazine (24 August 1981) praised Hwang's "gem of a play" for being "exquisitely balanced on the borderlines of history and fantasy, realism and symbolism, East and Westernization, speech and dance or mime, comedy and high seriousness . . . . It is as if every existential duality were encapsulated or suggested by this cunningly crafted yet somehow also ingenuous little play" (69).

The Dance and the Railroad garnered more awards for the Californian. Receiving the 1982 Chinese American Arts Council Award and a nomination for the New York Drama Desk Award as the best play of the season, the play subsequently was selected as part of ABC Television's Arts Cable Network "Theatre in America" series.

At the age of twenty-four, with two hit off-Broadway shows already to his credit and other scripts in the works, David Hwang withdrew from the Yale School of Drama and took up full-time residency in New York City. His earlier misgivings about the city gave way to enthusiasm for his work and his success. By the time of *Dance*'s Henry Street opening, Hwang already was developing play number three, a script actually begun before *Dance* but put on hold as the latter play commanded more of his creative energy. *Family Devotions*, a radical departure from the other plays, opened in Papp's Newman Theater just four months after *Dance*'s off-Broadway debut. The show was another southern California domestic drama.

The nine-character tragic farce focuses on three generations of an Asian-American family. The action runs continuously through two acts in the sunroom and on the adjoining tennis court of a well-to-do Asian-American couple. Wilbur is a Japanese-American married to Joanne, a Chinese-American. They reside with their daughter Jenny in Bel Air, the most elite, most pretentious, and most Caucasian of California communities. Nearby live Joanne's sister Hannah with her Chinese-American banker husband, Robert, and their violinist son, Chester, who is leaving to accept a position with the Boston Symphony. These six epitomize the realization of the California dream in its most garish extreme. Here we encounter refugees from the middle-class mores of Hwang's *FOB*, pushed up the "mountain of gold" by perseverance and a lust after Yankee materialism to the very pinnacle of Anglo-American luxury. The dramatist depicts all the vanity and gluttony of American capitalism exploited at the expense and obliteration of the Oriental cultural heritage. Exults Robert: "I was just an FOB. This American girl—she talked to me—asked me out—kissed me on the first date—and I thought, 'Land of Opportunity!' Anyway, I decided to turn my back on China. . . . This is my home. When I wanted to stop being a bum, make money, it let me. That's America!" (*Family Devotions*, in *Broken Promises* 133-34).

Offsetting these six characters, Hwang has inserted two elderly Chinese ladies who, though residents of the U.S. for years, have retained their language and their heritage through myths, stories, and memories now hazy and warped by time. The sisters, Ama and Popo, are the mothers of Joanne and Hannah respectively. Both live with Joanne and Wilbur in this Bel Air domain. Both are fiery "born-again" Evangelical Christians who deny their Chinese heritage before Aunt See-Goh-Poh, the family's first Christian and a Chinese missionary legend among her California relations. Spearheaded by Ama and Popo's Charismatic fervor, this household has become a living testimonial to God and See-Goh-Poh. Complete with rolling pulpit and flashing neon cross, the sunroom is regularly transformed into a family revival center. Witness and testimony in the tradition of See-Goh-Poh are mandatory daily fare.

As the play opens, all are awaiting the arrival of Ama and Popo's younger brother, Di-Gou, who for the past thirty years has remained in Communist China. His last visit to America was as a young medical intern at U.C.L.A. before returning to China and a successful medical practice. The sisters remember only Di-Gou at age eight, a mischievous boy saved from Hell-fire by a See-Goh-Poh miracle. Foremost in their minds this day is the hope that after years of Communist "brainwashing" Di-Gou still upholds the ideals of See-Goh-Poh.

The Di-Gou who finally arrives bears little resemblance to the Communist "ChinaMan" all had expected. Di-Gou is intelligent, glib, self-satisfied, and, to his sisters' shock, a total non-believer. He politely but forcefully rebukes the legend of See-Goh-Poh, the Christian "Woman Warrior." In fact, he has come to ask his sisters to renounce their faith and Western residence to return "home" with him. They counter his advances. As the first act closes, Ama—aboard her rolling, flashing pulpit—delivers a fiery testimony as the "Hallelujah Chorus" trumpets in the background.

Act Two, following immediately on the previous action, turns into grotesque daydream as Ama and Popo and their daughters assail Di-Gou and physically tie him to the table, while all chant the word of God and See-Goh-Poh into his face. In a scene of excruciating drama, Di-Gou breaks his bonds in a fit of holy possession and, speaking in tongues interpreted by the transfixed Chester, exposes the truth of See-Goh-Poh's missionary. Her crusade, attended by the boy Di-Gou, was only a ruse to conceal her unwanted pregnancy. The birth, at the boy's side, is exposed in graphic detail to the horror and denial of the sisters. Says Di-Gou: "Your stories are dead now that you know the truth" (163). In this macabre exorcism it is Di-Gou and the old ways which triumph over the New World myths—Ama and Popo literally "give up the ghost," collapsing and dying in their chairs as Di-Gou rants. In the wake of this catharsis both Di-Gou and young Chester, with whom he has found a kinship, depart. They leave a household in spiritual shambles, torn between the myth and reality, between the Chinese past and the California present. But Di-Gou, sadly, has learned as well. His parting realization, now that Ama and Popo are dead, is that "No one leaves America. And I desire only to drive an American car—very fast—down an American freeway" (167).

If *Family Devotions* leads audiences into a new arena for Hwang's confrontation-alienation drama, it is partly due to the writer-role model Sam Shepard's actual and peripheral influence on Hwang's scripting. The basics of this piece evolved after Hwang befriended Shepard and consciously experimented with variations on that Western playwright's intense dramatic style. In his own *Family Devotions*, we clearly see Hwang using elements from at least two of Shepard's menacingly surrealistic family dramas, *Curse of the Starving Class* (1977) and *Buried Child* (1978). Hwang presents here an Oriental "Curse-of-the-Starving-Class" family. An initial incident has Jenny searching for her lost "Chickie," mistaking a piece of fried chicken for its charred remains. In *Curse*, Emma hunts for a similar chicken. The Christian bigotry of Ama and Popo is reminiscent of that expounded by Shepard's "Halie" in *Buried Child*, a work which also holds the link to Hwang's treatment of Popo and Ama's passing away—in the form of Dodge's expiring in the Shepard play—and to the thematic evolution of the truth and its impact on the past. When the truth of See-Goh-Poh's "mission" is revealed to be not divine but carnal, this "buried child" revelation proves as catastrophic as that built into Shepard's opus. As provocative yet more poignant is the playwrights' shared view of a person's link to his lineage and its inextricable effect on his present existence. Says Vince in *Buried Child*, after his attempt to escape his family:

I was gonna run and keep right on running. . . . I could see myself in the windshield. My face. My eyes. I studied my face . . . as though I was looking at another man. As though I could see his whole race behind him. . . . His face became his father's face. . . . And his father's face changed to his Grandfather's face. And it went on like that. Changing. Clear on back to faces I'd never seen before but still recognized. Still recognized the bones underneath. (63)

In Hwang's play, as Di-Gou mirrors Chester's face in the back of the polished violin, he echoes Vince: "There are faces back further than you can see. Faces long before the white missionaries arrived in China. . . . Study your face and you will see—the shape of your face is the shape of faces back many generations . . . . You must become one with your family before you can hope to live away from it" (141). The young Hwang's artistic debt to Sam Shepard has been duly noted—the published script of *Family Devotions* Hwang dedicated to him.

Hwang's family, unlike Shepard's which functions comfortably amid derangement and perversion, seems suddenly to warp in confrontation and explode in a barrage of unanticipated theatrical fireworks. For his first large-cast show, Hwang has certainly developed a volatile ensemble. As before, we are given another battle between outsiders and insiders, between first and second generation Americans, between the truth, the perception, and the lie. Perhaps the most disturbing realization early in this play is that these families, Ama and Popo excluded, have lost all ethnic awareness. To borrow Hwang's term, these Asian-Americans exhibit an extreme form of "Bananaism": yellow outside, pure white within. They are named "Robert" and "Joanne." They collect tax shelters like trading cards. They are glaringly Anglicized. Hwang shows this well in the dilemma all have in remembering and trying to correctly pronounce "Di-Gou." It is an alien name from an alien culture.

Ama and Popo, for all their perceived Chinese-ness, are also hopelessly removed from the real China. They prefer to remain in a memory-enhanced Chinese fantasyworld wherein See-Goh-Poh eternally converts all of southeastern China to Christ. For them, the Communist Chinese homeland of Di-Gou is a circus of propagandistic stereotypes. "Communists. Make [Di-Gou] work in rice fields. . . . In rice field, all the people wear wires in their heads—yes!

Wires force them work all day and sing Communist song. . . . You wait till Di-Gou arrive. You will see. . . . Brainwash! You watch for little bit of wires in his hair" (109). When Robert is unable to find Di-Gou at the airport, Wilbur chides that he should have been able to find one old Chinese Man. Robert retorts, "Everyone on that plane was an old Chinese man!" "True," echoes Ama, "All Communist look alike" (123).

Into this world of myth and ignorance walks Di-Gou. He is beyond Hong Kong and Taiwan, beyond "FOB" caricatures, beyond the Lone actor on heartbreak mountain. He is Truth in the guise of a stalwart pagan from the Chinese present. He has come west to expose all—to expedite not only his sisters' recantations of their false prophet and Anglo-Christian ways, but also ultimately their anticipated return to the world of their ancestors, the proper Chinese world. In carrying through such intentions Hwang assaults the senses of the viewers. We watch heritage, values, customs, prejudices as they are batted and battered. As in Shepard, here too there must be casualties. Myths must be ripped apart for the truth to emerge. As Di-Gou leaves his sisters dead in the sunroom, he exits into America with the audience wondering if his musing, "No one leaves America," is truth or yet another myth. The play is haunting yet frustrating. It is not straightforward as *FOB* appears, nor lyrical as *The Dance*. Viewers are assaulted with severe portrayals, severe problems which linger with them as they leave the theater. The play ends with questions and few ready answers. Of his first three dramatic successes, it is this piece which has most confounded both Asian- and Euro-American theatergoers and critics.

In her "Foreword" to the *Broken Promises* collection, Maxine Hong Kingston articulates the confusion of many after sitting through *Family Devotions*. "The humor turns black. . . . The two most beguiling characters die suddenly and nightmarishly. Is this a warning? Is this what happens to a family that is warped by isolation? Is it time to stop hanging onto shreds of strange traditions somebody brought from China?" (ix). Countered Hwang, while discussing the work for *New York Daily News* writer Rob Baker, "For me, I don't believe it's possible to ever really leave a family. . . . Family devotion is in a person's blood—particularly for Asian-Americans, but probably for everyone" (M6).

There is much in this play that is superficially autobiographical. Robert is a wealthy banker and former kidnap victim with a violinist son. The violinist Hwang's father is a banker and former kidnap victim. Hwang's real family are, like this stage family, "born-again" Evangelical Christians and on one occasion did entertain a non-Christian Chinese relative. However, the visit bore little resemblance to the scripted nightmare. "I was raised in the Evangelical Christian Church," related Hwang to Lawrence Christon. "I question some of its specific tenets, but not the presence of the supernatural in everyday life. Some things people question don't strike me as strange at all. I grew up where someone could say, 'Oh yes, she died but we prayed for her and she came back to life' " (4). *Family Devotions* has undergone more rewriting than either of Hwang's earlier pieces, in part due to the complexity of plot elements coupled with family reaction to its relative autobiographical foundation. Hwang's father, moved to tears after *FOB*, "felt dizzy after *Family Devotions*. I felt as if my life had been turned upside down" (Gerard 89).

Family Devotions is a transition work for David Hwang, and an important step forward for the young dramatist. While *FOB* and *Dance* relied heavily on Oriental theatrical forms, *Devotions* is saturated with traditional Occidental farce. Perhaps *Los Angeles Times* critic Sylvie Drake assessed it best in her November 1981 column:

"Family Devotions" betrays considerable immaturity on the one hand and considerable daring on the other. . . . The serious attempt at the end to galvanize the mythology of the play is conceptually exciting, but misfires in the realization. There is every indication that Hwang will write this play well—or one like it—in about another five years. Right now, the grasp is still short of the reach. (43)

In fact, over the next five years Hwang did considerable reworking of this script. It has remained one of his most personal plays. Experiment or no, *Family Devotions* enjoyed a healthy 1981 run at Papp's Newman Theater, picking up along the way a second Drama Desk "Best Play" Award nomination for the twenty-four-year-old transplanted Californian.

In less than three years Hwang had developed from a Stanford senior writing and directing a play for campus competition, into an acclaimed international playwright and Asian-American theatrical voice. Within dramatic circles, David Henry Hwang was "hot." But with this celebrity status came a degree of frustration and self-doubt. He reflected in 1988 to Jeremy Gerard that "I was being put in a position for which I was not prepared. At 23 or 24, I was asked to be some sort of spokesperson for Asian-Americans on various issues which I hadn't really thought out. . . . It was no longer that I was a playwright per se, but that I was an Asian-American playwright, and my Asian-Americanness became the quality which defined me to the public" (89).

While the playwright truly enjoyed his success, two facts emerged which would color future projects. First, unlike several dramatists with whom he was now routinely grouped—Lanford Wilson and Christopher Durang among others—Hwang had never experienced the struggles most new playwrights endure to get produced and to become established. He had not been obliged to hustle his plays from agent to agent, producer to producer, and he had not had to refine his talent through years of off-off, and off-Broadway venues, as is the norm. Hwang broke into the New York theater scene quickly and successfully, but without the needed perspective such theatrical apprenticeships normally supply. If he was to grow as a playwright, he first had to step back and reevaluate his writings, his recognition, his reputation, and his goals. Only then could he make intelligent decisions about his future.

The second fact that would color his future career resulted to an extent from such self-evaluation. As noted earlier, Hwang realized that he was becoming typed as specifically an Asian-American writer and spokesperson, and while he would never turn his back on Asian-America, his survival depended now on expanding his scope to the non-Anglo Orient and to the non-Asian Occident. His realizations led him into a series of consciously diverse undertakings. "I basically want to give myself as much freedom as I can," he told Richard Stayton. "That means having access to all sorts of different media, film and TV as well as stage. And it means being able to write about a variety of topics" (E10).

Hwang's growing reputation and his close friendship with producer Joseph Papp won him a Rockefeller Grant as 1983 playwright-in-residence at the Public Theater. This post offered the freedom needed to experiment with several new ideas. The first of these experiments Papp presented on 21 October 1983: two Japan-inspired one-acts under the title *Sound and Beauty*. After the big-cast, high-power fireworks of *Family Devotions*, Hwang had returned to the two-character intimacy of *Dance*. Yet, unlike that show, these two pieces had Japanese settings, characters, and storylines. In both "The House of Sleeping Beauties" and "The Sound of a Voice," as the individual plays are called, Hwang shows the insider dealing with an outsider, and he develops the relationship which evolves

31

in each case. Here, however, the insiders are both women who are sought by the male intruders. Too, their arena is not the Asian-American West. Instead we are carried to an otherworldly Tokyo house of pleasure and to a mystical corner of a remote Japanese forest, respectively. The dramatist has returned to a favorite theme, the relationship of myth and the supernatural to our waking world, but the approach and the vehicle are decidedly new.

"The House of Sleeping Beauties" is a fantasy based on a tale of the same name by Japanese writer Yasunari Kawabata whose puzzling suicide in 1972 has intrigued Hwang. In this play, an elderly Kawabata visits a surreal, mystical pleasure house and develops an almost spiritual relationship with the equally aged proprietress. The play is fascinating in its four scenes, the first two divided from the others by several months in 1972. It begins with the character Kawabata being interviewed by his hostess, Michiko, to establish his suitability for her "sleeping beauties." He proves his worthiness and becomes a guest of the house. Yet, having sought the house to use it as a setting for a novelette, the writer later abandons his work in favor of the platonic peacefulness he experiences at Michiko's side. Initially a frequent visitor to the house, he becomes a live-in guest. The one-act ends with Hwang's version of Kawabata's suicide by poison, as the old man is rocked into eternal sleep cradled in Michiko's lap.

Most critics were either confused or disappointed by the uniqueness of this piece. It was so unlike the dramatist's previous plays that this unsettled several of them. "House" is a two-character drama, yet one in which themes of age versus youth are expanded. Counter to elderly characters from *Family Devotions*, are Kawabata and Michiko who seem endowed with the wisdom, vision, and maturity of long, introspective lives. Unlike the longer opus, "House" is not hurried. Like a piece of Japanese Noh Theater, it flows leisurely yet surely toward its inevitable conclusion. While conceived by a Westerner, this work possesses an essentially Oriental heart. It is this contradiction which set the New York critics at odds.

As a companion to "The House of Sleeping Beauties" the playwright created the better-received short play, "The Sound of a Voice." This tale, also a Japanese pas de deux, benefited from the acting of veteran John Lone as the "Man" (Natsuko Ohama starred as the "Woman"). Lone directed both plays. Hwang has described "Sound" as a traditional Japanese fable about a "warrior who goes into the woods to kill a witch and winds up falling in love with her." Though it feels authentic, Hwang actually made it up. "A lot of the witch's actions are open to interpretation, but it's also a modern story. It says: 'If you go into a relationship with a paranoid attitude, everything in it will turn to evil' " (Christon 4). While Lone was the director of choice for both shows, there appeared no suitable acting part for him. The Woman in "Sound" Hwang originally wrote as a Japanese *onnagata* role. In Japanese Kabuki Theater all female characters are acted by men specializing in women's parts, called *onnagata*. Hwang went so far as to offer the role to the great Kabuki actor Bando Tamasaboro, who, though interested, was already committed to other projects. Lone, who had acted female roles as a boy with the Peking Opera, another all-male domain, considered the part but also declined. Only after he was unable to cast a suitable *onnagata* did Hwang settle on actress Natsuko Ohama. Lone took the warrior role when the original actor left the show in rehearsals. Critical praise for Lone was again unanimous, while that for Ohama was fleeting. In Hwang's view the *onnagata* could have given the role a power that was lacking in Ohama. The playwright was convinced that that special *onnagata* talent would be a boon to this sort of role and a hit with Occidental audiences. In spite of mixed reviews, *Sound and Beauty* sold out a run which was twice extended.

On the one hand, these two new one-acts have nothing to do with Hwang's established Asian-American West. They are Japanese. They are conspicuously Oriental. On the other hand, they are crucial to Hwang's West. The New American West is one in which the majority shareholders are Japanese, Chinese, Vietnamese, and Korean, and to not attempt an understanding of these traditions, particularly for an Asian-American like Hwang, is to be as alienated from the world as the characters in *Family Devotions*. The New West has become a cultural crazy-quilt of Oriental and Occidental peoples and customs. A journey to Asia sheds light on the New American West. For Hwang such a journey led back to Los Angeles and a renewed commitment to familiar themes.

After the success of *Sound and Beauty* in New York, Hwang traveled through Europe back to Asia and then to Canada. In Toronto he met Chinese-Canadian actress Ophelia Chong. The two were married in Los Angeles in 1985. Hwang and his bride chose L.A. over New York as their permanent residence. His reestablished California base allowed the writer to better expand into television and multi-media projects which could complement his playwriting. A pet project of his became the development of a TV pilot for a situation comedy series inspired by *Family Devotions*. The pilot and sample episodes were well-received by the network, though none as yet has made it into programming.

A second television project, co-written with Frederic Kimball, reached the air in September 1985. The play, *Blind Alleys*, was commissioned by the Boston-based *Metromedia Playhouse* drama series, and produced and performed at WCVB's Boston studios. For the story Hwang again returns to a Los Angeles setting—this time a family-owned bowling alley. Fran, a white, had married Kenji, a Japanese-American, twenty years before. The marriage ended in divorce. Kenji fled, leaving the business to be run by Fran and by Kenji's Anglo ex-Army buddy, Woody. The plot twists when Kenji and Fran's daughter Amy, who looks more Japanese than Caucasian, announces her engagement to an Anglo boy and wishes to find her long-lost father to invite him to the wedding. The volatile Kenji attends the wedding and confronts the rural, bigoted parents of the groom. Cloris Leachman and Pat Morita fared well as Fran and Kenji on screen. The theme of bigotry and racial misunderstanding in the West was well-conceived, though in the scenes involving Kenji, Amy, and the groom's parents, the characters seemed grossly overdrawn. The effort was nevertheless a good one for Hwang, allowing him both media experimentation and prime-time exposure.

In early 1986, Hwang was asked by the Los Angeles Theatre Center to write a one-act to serve as a new companion to the Los Angeles premiere of "Sound of a Voice." The result was an entertaining, if not monumental, opus called "As the Crow Flies." In Los Angeles, a black woman has two identities. An employed domestic to an elderly Chinese lady, she later becomes a sort of "angel of death" who prepares her mistress for the netherworld. The Chinese lady speaks to spirits and seems afraid of nothing. As the black servant transforms into the heavenly harbinger, she ultimately guides her charge offstage, into the shadow of the descending crow. As in earlier attempts, Hwang further explores the boundaries between myth and reality, between the tangible and the intangible. Paired with "Sound of a Voice" this opus provided an interesting insight into a playwright in transition.

"A Theater Prodigy Exorcises His Roots and Moves On." Alex Witchel's leader to his David Hwang interview touted the premiere of *Rich Relations*. In this May 1986 *Elle Magazine* profile, Hwang called his new two-acter "a comedy about an American family dealing with the issue of resurrection" (46). Witchel's headline was prophetic. Hwang's first major work since *Family Devotions* nearly five years earlier opened off-Broadway at The Second Stage on 21 April 1986. It was both a critical and a financial flop—Hwang's first genuine failure. Though also his first all-Caucasian script, the non-Asian aspects of this piece proved moot to its real dramatic flaws, as articulated by *New York Times* critic Frank Rich in his April 22nd review and agreed upon by a majority of New York's theater patrons.

> At first glance, "Rich Relations," . . . would seem a radical departure from its author's previous work. . . . Yet once "Rich Relations" gathers steam . . . it seems much more consistent with the playwright's canon than superficial appearances might suggest. Like the wealthy, assimilated Chinese-American family in "Family Devotions," the family in the new play lives in Los Angeles, flirts with Evangelical Christianity and spends altogether too much time worshipping the false gods of materialism. . . .

> All of which goes to explain why "Rich Relations" seems so tired. . . . Mr. Hwang's credible but bland Caucasians exist mainly as pawns in a kneejerk authorial morality play pitting . . . the redemptive magic of religion against the American shrines of microwave ovens and "state of the art" audio-video equipment. (C15)

What happened to "the prodigy"? Hwang's use of an all-Anglo cast was a laudable, necessary step forward, but these white players are perceived merely as *Family Devotions* clones. Asian-Americans could step into these roles and not alter the playwright's dramatic themes. This "new" play is a tentative, anemic, and caricatured cousin to the older drama.

This "comedy" is set in the recreation room of a luxurious home high in the hills, a spectacular view of Los Angeles below. It is *Family Devotions'* Bel Air estate transported to the top of *Dance's* "mountain of gold." High-tech conveniences litter a set dominated by a huge television. We meet Hinson, a millionaire real estate developer and high-tech junkie, as he plays with a telephone which receives through his TV speakers. He has three car phones and the materialistic lust of *Devotions'* Robert and Wilbur taken to nearly allegorical extremes. Into this house of mammon walks Hinson's twenty-nine-year-old son Keith, a debate coach at an exclusive Eastern girls' prep school, with his sixteen-year-old, former-student girlfriend, Jill. The guilt-laden son has left his employer an incriminating written confession exposing his several sexual escapades with former students. Such a letter, Keith realizes, will no doubt bar him from any future teaching positions. He has just driven 3,000 miles, with his runaway companion, to seek asylum in his father's Western abode on the hillside. So far Hwang's plot is promising. Yet instead of focusing on this dilemma for his central conflict, Hwang retreats to the comfort of his "born-again," salvation-resurrection themes, and *Rich Relations* loses both momentum and originality.

> I had TB [Hinson explains]. Doctors said, "No hope," but
> I prayed to God, "Save my life and I will be a shining
> light for thee." I thought I was dead, but then I saw this
> light—aaaah!—so bright. And this hand reached out to me.
> When I took it, it was not a ghost but one of my sisters.
> Then I knew—God had answered my prayers. (19)

Hinson was divinely plucked from the dead to become the "Reverend Ike" of Hollywood real estate. Hinson's mother and sister, Barbara, feel directly responsible for this resurrection, as Barbara continuously reminds. But Keith has turned away from the church and Jill is a non-believer. Here too is a potentially powerful reworking of a favorite Hwang motif. Yet as such a reworking appears imminent, the dramatist balks, sidetracked by Barbara's intrusion.

Hwang molds Barbara into the plain, unworldly antithesis of Hinson. She vehemently pursues her brother's complete return to his pastorship, just as she seeks a goodly share of his money. Barbara's auto-mechanic husband Fred, like herself a devout Charismatic Christian, is having a live-in affair with "Bonnie"—with his wife's approval. The trio on occasion even share the same bed! The last player in this unlikely morality play is Fred and Barbara's daughter Marilyn, an overly made-up, underachieving "Mary Magdalene" whom Barbara insists on forcing in marriage to cousin Keith, as a way to bilk money out of her "rich relations." To force her hand, Barbara mounts the outside balcony railing and threatens to jump if the two are not wedded. With this dilemma and several unanswered questions, Act One ends.

Act Two continues the previous action and proceeds into a torrid explanation of Barbara's financial fanaticism. Empathetic Jill joins her on the rail as Hinson returns home, calls his sister's bluff, and coerces her off the rail where Jill remains. Captivated by the TV, Marilyn pushes its volume louder and louder, drowning her mother's proselytizing and her uncle's hymn singing. At the peak of reverie the TV explodes, and the house plunges into darkness and silence. When light returns, Jill has disappeared. Now Marilyn takes a turn on the perch. Jill, found by Keith at the bottom of the hill, is "all crumpled, eyes looking up" (76). Why she jumped, or whether she jumped, remains unclear. The time is now ripe for Hwang's "issue of resurrection," though any hope of "resurrecting" a successful drama is here dashed by weak Shepard parody and an absence of rationale for the desired denouement. Keith wants Hinson to use his old Charismatic powers to literally resurrect Jill. Inner turmoil bubbles into physical conflict escalating into a melee with golf clubs, god's gladiators symbolically smashing appliances instead of each other. Mother and daughter recount Hinson's rise from the dead in a scene weakly reminiscent of the Di-Gou and Chester revelation in *Devotions*. Barbara in her zeal pushes Marilyn off her rail where she surrealistically levitates. The appliances shut off and the room again is darkened. Only Marilyn, afloat in the evening light, is visible. She intones Hwang's message—a wonderful monologue, sadly incoherent within its dramatic medium.

> Listen—can you hear it? Behind every noise in the city, every sound we've learned to make, behind the clatter of our streets, the hum of turbines, the roar of electricity—behind all this, there is a constant voice. A voice which carries hope from beyond the grave . . . . It is a voice which lurks behind every move we make. To listen to it—is to rage against the grave, we save our souls, we bring ourselves back from the dead. (85)

The lights go out, and when they return Jill is back on the balcony unscathed. Marilyn enters looking for her. As the two exit together, Jill chastises Keith with the observation that resurrection "shouldn't be that hard" (89). Keith and Hinson, left alone on the balcony, place ears to the ground to presumably listen for that "voice which carries hope from beyond the grave." They do not seem to hear it as the play ends—neither does the audience.

Rich Relations sports the look and feel of a first play by an ambitious beginner. This is a piece loaded with loose ends and unrealized potential that, with serious rethinking and rewriting, could become powerful theater. If its creator were to concentrate on his built-in conflict of materialism versus spiritualism among the California rich, using Keith's crisis of conscience and Hinson's addiction to material wealth as hooks, and Jill and Barbara as character foils, *Rich Relations* could extend rather than parody the spiritual metaphor set in *Family Devotions* and could fortify the real dichotomy of themes into a significant treatment of that omnipresent by-product of the California suburban experience. Hwang was not a beginner but a young playwright mired in other concerns. Ideas of resurrection and spiritual dependence haunted him as he fought back from a temporary case of writer's block. The cure took the form of the *Rich Relations* script. With this script, as Alex Witchel proclaimed, Hwang "Exorcised his roots" in deference to his dramatic instincts. The failure of this play at the box-office, said Hwang, liberated him and finally allowed him to move beyond his family devotions and his rich relations to a theatrical plateau of extraordinary originality and sophistication.

On 11 May 1986, *The New York Times* published a news story relating the outcome of a bizarre French spy trial, under the head, "France Jails Two in Odd Case of Espionage." Correspondent Richard Bernstein reported that Bernard Bouriscot, a former French diplomat at one time attached to France's embassy in Peking, and a Mr. Shi Peipu, a once-popular Chinese Peking Opera star, had both been sentenced to six years in prison for passing more than 150 French documents to a Communist Chinese agent. While most of the information was inconsequential, Mr. Bouriscot's public notoriety in Parisian circles was caused not by his espionage conviction, but by the incredible circumstances which evoked it.

According to the transcripts, Mr. Bouriscot met Mr. Shi in 1964, when Bouriscot was attached to Peking's French Embassy and Shi was an actor with the Peking Opera, specializing in the traditionally male-performed women's roles (the Peking equivalent to the Japanese *onnagata*). Bouriscot thought Shi was actually female, the actor apparently doing nothing to dispel the illusion; and a love affair ignited which lasted twenty years. At one point Shi announced "she" was pregnant by Bouriscot and several months later showed him his Eurasian "son" christened Shi Dudu. The amazing case was exposed in 1983, when Shi and Shi Dudu left mainland China to reside in Paris with Bouriscot, who incredibly still believed the two to be mother and son. Shi's change of residence alerted French counterespionage agents who subsequently questioned Bouriscot about his activities with the Chinese. Bouriscot confessed to his crimes and explained the reasons behind such involvement. According to the report, it was only during his trial that he finally learned Shi was a he. Asked by the judge to account for his astonishing ignorance, the Frenchman reportedly replied: "I was shattered to learn that he is a man, but my conviction remains unshakable that for me at that time he was really a woman and was the first love of my life. And then there was the child that I saw, Shi Dudu. He looked like me." Additionally, the lovers' trysts were always short and usually carried out in darkness. Rationalized Bouriscot on Shi: "He was very shy . . . I thought it was a Chinese custom" (K7).

When Hwang read this account, he was tantalized by the theatrical potential of its sexual and racial incongruities. The dramatic implications of Bouriscot's tale appeared numerous. Said Hwang to Jeremy Gerard, "The story was like a perfect little jar that could hold all these different subjects" (44). Hwang gave this project his total artistic attention. By October, a polished first draft, titled *M. Butterfly*, was completed. In fleshing out the script, the dramatist had had to wrestle with two major artistic problems. First, he needed a hook, a dramatic angle which would take this off-beat spy trial out of the courtroom and make it theatrically interesting. Second, he had to deal credibly with the paramount question—How could Mr. Bouriscot have a twenty-year, intimate affair with Shi Peipu without dicovering Shi was not female? "One day," Hwang told Gerard, "it popped into my head: What did Bouriscot think he was getting? Well, he probably thought he was getting Madame Butterfly." For Hwang growing up in southern California, Madame Butterfly existed only as a cultural stereotype. "Like, sometimes you would say, 'Oh, she's pulling a Butterfly'—which meant someone trying to do a submissive-Oriental number" (44). This strange tale afforded the playwright a perfect vehicle for treating personal concerns about racism, sexism, Yankee imperialism, and broad inherent misconceptions in East/West relations.

Composer Philip Glass, with whom Hwang had previously collaborated, referred the author to Broadway producer Stuart Ostrow, who, intrigued by *M. Butterfly*'s possibilities, financed further research and rewriting. Though Hwang retained the real names in his first draft, he subsequently renamed his characters. Bouriscot and Shi became "Rene Gallimard" and "Song Liling." The scatological-sounding Dudu, was humorously rechristened "Song Peepee." The finished play was mailed to British director John Dexter, a Broadway success with *Equus* in 1975, who loved the script and agreed to direct its Broadway production. The play was given the most lavish staging of the season, at a cost of 1.5 million dollars. After a brief preview at Washington's National Theater, *M. Butterfly* opened at the O'Neill Theater, 20 March 1988, to overall ecstatically positive reviews. The play was well-attended, the Broadway audiences encouraging.

When the theater critics announced the annual Drama Desk Awards in May, Hwang's work was the big winner among dramas. Dexter won for Best Director, and B.D. Wong for Best Featured Actor (as Song Liling), while *M. Butterfly* itself was voted the year's Outstanding New Play. One week later, when the prestigious Tony Award nominations were announced, *Butterfly* again was the leader with seven nominations. At the Tony Awards presentation on June 5th, Dexter and Wong again won as best Director and Featured

Actor respectively. *M. Butterfly* was once more voted Best Play on Broadway. The work subsequently received the Outer Critics Circle Award for Best Broadway Play and the John Gassner Award for the Best New American Play. What had Hwang done in transforming a curious news event into the most heralded drama of 1988? How did he incorporate his East/West themes into a plot so unlike any he had previously created?

David Hwang's most astute artistic decision was in not trying to simulate a realistic, chronologically ordered scenario. An epic tale spanning two decades and two continents, wherein all but the sketchiest of details were unknown, would be nearly impossible to compress into two hours on the stage. Instead, he employed a "memory play" approach, rendering his dramatic episodes through a series of scenic flashbacks narrated by the convicted Frenchman from his jail cell. This structure, reminiscent of those employed by Peter Shaffer in *Equus* and Tom Stoppard in *Travesties*, allows the protagonist to selectively relive the meaningful events of his twenty-year romance as he perceives them. Perception, not truth, prevails as the working catalyst herein for playwright and protagonist; and, perhaps more crucially, it allows the protagonist to address from the outset the implausibility of his gender misidentification. Only ten minutes elapse before Gallimard throws the issue at the audience. The scene is a Paris party, where the absent lover is the butt of derision:

WOMAN: He still claims not to believe the truth.

MAN 2: (*Laughing*) He says . . . it was dark . . . and she was very modest!

MAN 1: So — What? He never touched her with his hands?

MAN 2: Perhaps he did, and simply misidentified the equipment. A compelling case for sex education in the schools. (2)

But the Gallimard who presents the scene remains steadfast. "Can they really be so foolish?" he muses. "Men like that—they should be scratching at my door, begging to learn my secrets! For I, Rene Gallimard, you see, I have known and been loved by . . . the Perfect Woman" (2). The overriding dilemma has been shoved to the forefront, and Hwang is now free to begin twisting his plot around its *Madame Butterfly* parallels.

For Gallimard, fantasizing Puccini's less-than-heroic Lt. Pinkerton— "not very good-looking, not too bright, and pretty much a wimp" (2)—this opera provides the perfect feminine ideal. "Cio-Cio-San," the Oriental "Butterfly," gives up everything for her American master. Pinkerton mercilessly abandons her for America, even after she has borne him a child. His actions force her suicide. Indeed, what first attracts Gallimard to the singer is Song Liling's powerful rendering of the *Madame Butterfly* death scene at an embassy gathering. This fantastic operatic parallel to the real events of the Bouriscot affair seems perfectly congruent in the creative hands of the playwright. All Gallimard can see in Song's character is the beauty and pure sacrifice of the submissive Oriental when confronted by the power of the Occident. With this perception and Song's subsequent rebuttal, Hwang crystallizes the play's central confrontation, demonstrating Gallimard's essential ignorance of the Asian reality, and by extension that of most Occidentals. Song challenges Gallimard's cultural hypocrisy:

Consider it this way: What would you say if a blonde homecoming queen fell in love with a short Japanese businessman? He treats her cruelly, then goes home for three years, during which time she prays to his picture and turns down marriage from a young Kennedy. Then, when she learns he has remarried, she kills herself. Now, I believe you would consider this girl to be a deranged idiot, correct? But because it's an Oriental who kills herself for a Westerner—ah!—you find it beautiful. (4)

This Occidental/Oriental paradox is at the core of Gallimard's misconduct, and on a larger scale, also at the core of what Hwang purports to be the ultimate obstacle impeding East-West understanding and accommodation. As Hwang revealed to Gerard: "The play might be seen as anti-Western in the sense that it's saying that the West just has not looked at these issues. That's partly true, but it's very pro-American too. It's saying, 'These are the facts of the situation and if you would like to get along better in the world, then you had better look at the world more clearly. The East isn't going away' " (89). Gallimard never does seem to understand. By the start of Act Two, he is still rationalizing: "While we men may all want to kick Pinkerton, very few of us would pass up the opportunity to be Pinkerton" (8). It is Gallimard's Puccini-esque perceptions of Song and his world, that willful gullibility to take this opera-of-the-world at its face value—make-up, costumes, props, scripted action, and all its artifices—that allows him to become the incredibly pliable dupe of Song Liling and to maintain his delusion, in the wake of public ridicule, even after Song's male identity has been exposed.

What emerges from the contradictions is the haunting awareness of the power of illusion motivated by love. At the end we perceive, with the Frenchman, that the man who idolized Puccini's Pinkerton must accordingly share the fate of his Butterfly. This is a love story after all, not a spy thriller nor a historical slice-of-life, though elements of these permeate *M. Butterfly*. Finally, simply put, this has been a romance about "a man who loved a woman created by a man" (16).

> In public, I have continued to deny that Song Liling is a man. This brings me headlines. . . . But alone, in my

cell, I have long since faced the truth. . . . My mistakes were simple and absolute—the man I loved . . . deserved nothing but a kick in the behind, and instead I gave him . . . all my love.

Yes—love. Why not admit it all? That was my undoing, wasn't it? Love warped my judgment, blinded my eyes, rearranged the very lines on my face . . . until I could look in the mirror and see nothing but . . . a woman. (16)

Taking the play as a love story, what one finds amazing is the sheer textual variety of ideas and problems this script propagates. While fortifying layer upon layer of this East-West intrigue, David Hwang continuously invents ways to shake it down, turn the story inside out, playfully parody it, and openly satirize its Occidental mores with his Asian's-eye-view. Yet, when this former debate star has finished his intellectual and theatrical cross-examination, this riveting, tightly wound Broadway blockbuster is the result. It is as if all previous creation by the author was but preparation for *M. Butterfly*. The Gwan Gung/Fa Mu Lan sparring matches of *FOB*, the Peking Opera fantasy played out in the historical-political arena of *Dance*, the grim backlash of American affluence against Asian tradition, and of imagined China clashing against the real China, of *Family Devotions*, the sensual lure of the East of both "Sleeping Beauties" and "Sound of a Voice," and even the sacrifice-death-resurrection motif of *Rich Relations*—all seem to synthesize in *M. Butterfly*. This opus emerges as a masterwork of the global West, risen from the myths and metaphors of the American West.

David Henry Hwang has emerged as the first widely acclaimed, Broadway-produced Asian-American dramatist to capture the imagination of the Asian-American communities on both coasts, the international Asian arts contingents, and the non-Asian theater-going public. His short but meaningful theatrical apprenticeship, if it may be so called, from *FOB*'s success through *Rich Relations*' failure, readied the writer to develop both artistically and culturally, until his acclaim with *M. Butterfly* pronounced him one of the most distinctive stars on the dramatic horizon since Sam Shepard brought forth his Wild Western theaterworks.

David Hwang is clearly a writer of the American West. Yet his West is far removed from that traditionally brought to mind by the writings of Bret Harte or David Belasco. Hwang's West is that built with "coolie" labor in the mines and on the railroads from Omaha to Sacramento to San Francisco. His Westerner was ignored or ridiculed by early white society and is misunderstood by many today. Yet his Oriental Westerner has become a pivotal fixture in both the significant literature and the cultural re-examination of what has metamorphosed into the New American West. And as a portrayer of Asian-American heritage and heart-break on the American stage, his contribution has been immeasurable, as Maxine Hong Kingston says in praising him:

Chinese American actors are given too few dignified parts to play. If no playwrights like David Hwang came along, a generation of actors who speak our accents would be lost. A novelist can only invent an approximate orthography. For voices, the play's the thing. Chinese American theater, which started out with a bang—firecrackers, drums—keeps dying out. David Henry Hwang gives it life once again. (*Broken Promises* ix)

As a playwright drawing upon his heritage for his significant literary and aesthetic contributions, he joins the likes of other California-bred authors—Luis Valdez and William Saroyan among others—who likewise established international followings without sacrificing their ethnic integrity or their inborn cultural values. As a pure talent of the theater, Hwang has joined the elite of his craft. Particularly akin to other dynamic Western-inspired artists like Mark Medoff, Lanford Wilson, and Sam Shepard, Hwang possesses a vision, and an ability to convey that vision, which make him a unique, sought-after artist in the international theater world.

For the future? Hwang is at that point in his career where he can feel free to explore whatever subject matter, in whichever medium, he finds appealing. If, in so doing, he creates more challenging roles for Asian actors, Hwang will be pleased. In the world of David Henry Hwang, after all he has thus far achieved, the words of *FOB*'s Dale, in the end ring equally true for their author: "I've paid my dues. And that's why I am much better now. I'm making it, you know? I'm making it in America."

Selected Bibliography

HWANG'S PLAYS

"As the Crow Flies." Unpublished Manuscript, 1986.

Broken Promises: Four Plays. New York: Avon, 1983. (Includes: *FOB; The Dance and the Railroad; Family Devotions; The House of Sleeping Beauties;* plus a "Foreword" by Maxine Hong Kingston.)

The Dance and the Railroad (Abridged). *The Best Plays of 1981-1982.* Ed. Otis L. Guernsey, Jr. New York: Dodd, 1983.

The Dance and the Railroad (with Introduction). *The Best Short Plays of 1982.* Ed. Ramon Delgado. Radnor, PA: Chilton, 1982.

FOB. TCG/New Plays USA 1. Ed. James Leverett. New York: Theatre Communications Group, 1982.

M. Butterfly. American Theatre Magazine July/Aug. 1988: 1-16 (Insert).

Rich Relations. Unpublished Manuscript, 1986.

"The Sound of a Voice." New York: Dramatists Play Service, 1984.

WORKS CITED AND OTHER SECONDARY SOURCES

Auerbach, Doris. *Sam Shepard, Arthur Kopit, and the Off-Broadway Theater.* Boston: Twayne, 1982.

Baker, Rob. "The World of David Hwang." *New York Daily News* 1 Sept. 1981: M1 and 6.

Barnes, Clive. "Sex and Silk When East Meets West." *New York Post.* (rpt.) *The New York Theatre Critics' Reviews* 2 May 1988: 333-34.

Bernstein, Richard. "France Jails Two in Odd Case of Espionage." *The New York Times* 11 May 1986: K7.

Berson, Misha. "Buried Treasure." *The San Francisco Bay Guardian* 5 Aug. 1981: 13.

Browne, Andy. "Going Bananas over Bananas." *South China Morning Post* [Hong Kong] 2 Dec. 1982: 15.

Chin, Frank. *The Chickencoop Chinaman and The Year of the Dragon.* Seattle: U of Washington P: 1981.

Christon, Lawrence. "Playwright Balances Life's Improbabilities." *Los Angeles Times* 12 Feb. 1986: pt. VI, 1 and 4.

Colker, David. "He Laid Down the Law for the Theater." *Herald-Examiner* [Los Angeles] 14 Nov. 1981: B1 and 4.

Drake, Sylvie. "Hwang: L.A. Playwright Has a New York Dateline." *Los Angeles Times* 8 Nov. 1981: 43 and 46.

Feingold, Michael. "Obie Award: David Henry Hwang's Deathwatch." *The Village Voice* 11 Nov. 1983: 111.

——————. "Transformational Glamour." *The Village Voice* 29 Mar. 1988: 115 and 118.

Gerard, Jeremy. "David Hwang: Riding on the Hyphen." *The New York Times Magazine* 13 Mar. 1988: 44 and 88-89.

Henderson, Kathy. "A Rare Butterfly" *Playbill* July 1988: 8-12.

Hummler, Richard. "M. Butterfly." *Variety* 23 Mar. 1988: 126.

Hurley, Joseph. "David Hwang Fights the Big Lie." *The Soho News* 15 July 1981: 22.

Hwang, David. "Are Movies Ready for Real Orientals?" *The New York Times* 11 Aug. 1985: II, 1 and 21.

Kim, Elaine H. "Asian American Writers: A Bibliographical Review." *American Studies International* Oct. 1984: 41-78.

Kimmelman, Michael. "Broadway's New Realpolitik." *The New York Times* 22 May: II, 1 and 8.

Kingston, Maxine Hong. *China Men.* New York: Ballantine, 1981.

——————. *The Woman Warrior: Memoirs of a Girlhood Among Ghosts.* New York: Random, 1976.

Nightingale, Benedict. *Fifth Row Center: A Critic's Year on and off Broadway.* New York: Times Books, 1986.

Oliver, Edith. "East and West." *The New Yorker* 21 Nov. 1983: 209-10.

——————. "East in the West." *The New Yorker* 16 June 1980: 96-97.

——————. "Off Broadway." *The New Yorker* 27 July 1981: 52.

——————. "Poor Butterfly." *The New Yorker* 4 Apr. 1988: 12.

_____. "Poor Butterfly." *The New Yorker* 4 Apr. 1988: 12.

Pace, Eric. "'I Write Plays to Claim a Place for Asian-Americans.'" *The New York Times* 12 July 1981: 4D.

Reiter, Susan. "New Territory for David Hwang." *New York Daily News* 23 Oct. 1983: 5 and 8.

Rich, Frank. "'Dance, Railroad,' By David Henry Hwang." *The New York Times* 31 Mar. 1981: C7.

_____. "'M. Butterfly,' A Story of a Strange Love, Conflict and Betrayal." *The New York Times* 21 Mar. 1988: C10.

_____. "'Rich Relations' From David Hwang." *The New York Times* 22 Apr. 1986: C15.

Shepard, Sam. *Angel City, Curse of the Starving Class and Other Plays.* New York: Urizen, 1976.

_____. *Buried Child.* New York: Urizen, 1979.

Shewey, Don. "His Art Blends the Best of Two Cultures on Stage." *The New York Times* 30 Oct. 1983: H6.

Simon, John. "David Hwang's *Rich Relations* Is a Poor Work for an Able Playwright to Perpetrate." *New York Magazine* 5 May 1986: 90.

Stayton, Richard. "Playwright Is a Bicoastal Success." *Herald-Examiner* [Los Angeles] 11 Dec. 1983: E10.

Stein, Ruthe. "Asian-American Life Provides His Plots." *San Francisco Chronicle* 13 Oct. 1981: 22-23.

Watt, Douglas. "'Dance and the Railroad' Is Right on Track." *New York Daily News* 17 July 1981: M6.

Weiner, Bernard. "Two Writers Face Dilemma of Being Minorities in Mainstream." *San Francisco Sunday Examiner/Chronicle* 22 Feb. 1987: 38.

Wilson, Edwin. "Theater: Of Relations Erotic and Diplomatic." *The Wall Street Journal* 22 Mar. 1988: 32.

Witchel, Alex. "A Theater Prodigy Exorcises His Roots and Moves On." *Elle Magazine* May 1986: 46.